The Gratitude for Busine

MW00900452

Want to grow your business the easy and relaxed way?

Find more things to be grateful for in your business.

It's that simple.

And yes, gratitude is a business strategy.

With gratitude, teams grow, ideal clients are attracted (and they stay), the right business partners are drawn to you and all roads lead to a healthy and growing bank account!

The Gratitude for Business Journal

Here's why it works.

"The more gratefully we fix our minds on the Supreme power when good things come to us, the more good things we will receive, and the more rapidly they will come. The reason for this is simply that the mental attitude of gratitude draws the mind into closer touch with the source from which the blessings come."

Wallace D Wattles - The Science of Getting Rich

I have used gratitude as an integral part of creating my own success and I also coach my clients to keep a journal just for documenting things they are grateful for each day in their business. When you focus on current things in your business to be grateful for, simultaneously a momentum of expanded results that defies human logic begins to occur also.

Go ahead. Enjoy 30 days of giving some love and gratitude to your business. Experience the power of gratitude!

To Your Success,

Tasha Chen

ScienceOfGettingRichAcademy.com

The Gratitude for Business Journal

Set Your Intention

_____

_____

_____

_____

_____

_____

_____

_____

_____

_____

_____

_____

_____

Gratitude Oil

Gratitude essential oil blend is formulated to help us to connect with the essence of the experience of gratitude. Gratitude is the highest measurable emotion with Love the only one above it but, Love is not able to be measured. The more we are able to consistently maintain a higher vibration, the more balanced we are, the more we are able to focus and visualize our heart's desires.

In The Science of Getting Rich Academy, we are taught that the energy of Gratitude is one that is integral to the experience of manifesting. When we journal daily, we express gratitude for all things, from finding a penny to receiving $1000, and it raises our vibration, the way we feel in our skin or the way we feel in our relationship with ourselves. Again, the higher our vibration the more in balance we are, the more we are able to focus and the more we are able to successfully manifest our heart's desires.

And when we are not in the best frame of mind, our energy or vibration drops and we lose our ability to focus and this affects our ability to manifest. When we are in this state of being, focusing on what we are grateful for raises our vibration very quickly. Using 1-2 drops of Gratitude essential oil before we begin our gratitude journal helps us to raise our vibration even more rapidly and re-application as needed helps us to keep our vibration higher, enhancing our ability to focus and visualize thereby enhancing our ability to manifest.

We recommend this special Gratitude Oil to use when journaling.

Visit www.tashachen.com/Gratitude to purchase your very own bottle!

The Gratitude for Business Journal

Instructions

1   Use each day's prompt as inspiration for your gratitude journaling.

2   Journal gratitude for what currently exists in your business as well as what you wish to create. For example, express gratitude for your current clients as well as the large number of future clients coming your way.

3   If a prompt is NOT currently relevant to you, journal gratitude for it being your reality in the future. For example, you may not currently have excess funds for investments from your business, however you can still journal "I am so grateful my business generates excess funds that allows me to invest in several passive income creating opportunities"

4   EVIDENCE - At the end of this Journal are blank pages for you to Document Evidence. As you go through the 30 days many good things will begin to happen in your life and business, be sure to document these occurrences and celebrate the proof that your vibration is raising and as you begin attracting "more good things".

Day 1

My People

Clients I get to serve in business

My clients are grateful for my consideration, care and time. They realize there is very little I won't do for them, and that I will always go the extra mile for them. They know I have their backs, often putting their needs ahead of my own. They know they can COUNT ON ME and have the freedom to focus on their businesses and building them because of this fact. They send referrals to me and are confident that the referrals will be protected and looked after in a similarly caring & protective way. They know I'm focused on so much more than $!

The Gratitude for Business Journal

Day 2

My Product

Skills, talents, expertise, physical product

_____

_____

_____

_____

_____

_____

_____

_____

_____

_____

_____

_____

_____

_____

_____

Day 3

My Money

Making a living from my business

_____

_____

_____

_____

_____

_____

_____

_____

_____

_____

_____

_____

_____

Day 4

My Partners & Collaborators

_____

_____

_____

_____

_____

_____

_____

_____

_____

_____

_____

_____

_____

Day 5

My Team

_____

_____

_____

_____

_____

_____

_____

_____

_____

_____

_____

_____

_____

Day 6

My Personal Development

_____

_____

_____

_____

_____

_____

_____

_____

_____

_____

_____

_____

_____

_____

_____

Day 7

Systems & Technology That Support My Business

_____

_____

_____

_____

_____

_____

_____

_____

_____

_____

_____

_____

_____

_____

_____

The Gratitude for Business Journal

Day 8

Client Results & Testimonials

_____

_____

_____

_____

_____

_____

_____

_____

_____

_____

_____

_____

_____

Day 9

Investments Made & To Be Made

_____

_____

_____

_____

_____

_____

_____

_____

_____

_____

_____

_____

_____

_____

Day 10

Client Referrals

_____

_____

_____

_____

_____

_____

_____

_____

_____

_____

_____

_____

_____

Day 11

Spiritual Beliefs That Support Me In Business

_____

_____

_____

_____

_____

_____

_____

_____

_____

_____

_____

_____

_____

_____

_____

_____

Day 12

My Social Network

_____

_____

_____

_____

_____

_____

_____

_____

_____

_____

_____

_____

_____

Day 13

Vacations On My Terms

_____

_____

_____

_____

_____

_____

_____

_____

_____

_____

_____

_____

_____

_____

_____

_____

Day 14

Flexible Work Hours

_____

_____

_____

_____

_____

_____

_____

_____

_____

_____

_____

_____

_____

_____

Day 15

Future Results

_____
_____
_____
_____
_____
_____
_____
_____
_____
_____
_____
_____
_____
_____

Day 16

Past Failures & Lessons Learned

_____

_____

_____

_____

_____

_____

_____

_____

_____

_____

_____

_____

_____

Day 17

Coaches & Mentors

_____

_____

_____

_____

_____

_____

_____

_____

_____

_____

_____

_____

_____

_____

_____

The Gratitude for Business Journal

Examples Of Success To Model

_____
_____
_____
_____
_____
_____
_____
_____
_____
_____
_____
_____
_____

Day 19

Clarity

_____

_____

_____

_____

_____

_____

_____

_____

_____

_____

_____

_____

_____

_____

Day 20

Infinite Opportunities To Grow

_____

_____

_____

_____

_____

_____

_____

_____

_____

_____

_____

_____

_____

_____

_____

Day 21

Faith & Belief In Massive Success

_____

_____

_____

_____

_____

_____

_____

_____

_____

_____

_____

_____

_____

_____

Day 22

Marketing That Creates Expansion

_____

_____

_____

_____

_____

_____

_____

_____

_____

_____

_____

_____

_____

Day 23

New Product Ideas That Generate Easy Revenue

_____

_____

_____

_____

_____

_____

_____

_____

_____

_____

_____

_____

_____

_____

_____

Day 24

All Levels Of Success Achieved

_____

_____

_____

_____

_____

_____

_____

_____

_____

_____

_____

_____

_____

Day 25

Relationships Made Through Business

_____

_____

_____

_____

_____

_____

_____

_____

_____

_____

_____

_____

_____

_____

Day 26

All Evidence That Success Is Coming

_____

_____

_____

_____

_____

_____

_____

_____

_____

_____

_____

_____

_____

_____

Day 27

Profits

_____

_____

_____

_____

_____

_____

_____

_____

_____

_____

_____

_____

_____

_____

Day 28

Leadership Skills

_____

_____

_____

_____

_____

_____

_____

_____

_____

_____

_____

_____

_____

Day 29

Financial Freedom Created From Business

_____

_____

_____

_____

_____

_____

_____

_____

_____

_____

_____

_____

_____

_____

Day 30

Future Value Of My Business

_____

_____

_____

_____

_____

_____

_____

_____

_____

_____

_____

_____

_____

_____

Evidence

_____

_____

_____

_____

_____

_____

_____

_____

_____

_____

_____

_____

Evidence

_____

_____

_____

_____

_____

_____

_____

_____

_____

_____

_____

Evidence

_____

_____

_____

_____

_____

_____

_____

_____

_____

_____

_____

The Gratitude for Business Journal

Evidence

_____

_____

_____

_____

_____

_____

_____

_____

_____

_____

_____

_____

_____

Evidence

_____

_____

_____

_____

_____

_____

_____

_____

_____

_____

_____

_____

92595059R00024

Made in the USA
Middletown, DE
09 October 2018